Secrets of the VAMPIRE

To our dark sides... and, as always, to our wonderful editor, Chloé.

Text by Julie Légère and Elsa Whyte
Illustrations by Laura Pérez

First published in the US in 2023 by Wide Eyed Editions,
an imprint of The Quarto Group.
100 Cummings Center, Suite 265D, Beverly, MA 01915, US.
T +1 978-282-9590 F +1 078-283-2742 **www.Quarto.com**

First published in France under the title:
Secrets de vampires

A CIP record for this book is available from the Library of Congress.

ISBN 978-0-7112-8507-1
eISBN 978-0-7112-8938-3

The illustrations were created digitally
Set in Scala and Gaudy

Published by Debbie Foy
Edited by Alex Hithersay
Translated by Amber Husain
Designed by Lyli Feng
Production by Dawn Cameron

Manufactured in Guangdong, China CC042023
9 8 7 6 5 4 3 2 1

JULIE LÉGÈRE

ELSA WHYTE

LAURA PÉREZ

A SUPERNATURAL SOURCEBOOK
OF OUR LEGEND AND LORE

WIDE EYED EDITIONS

"The bats have left the bell tower
The victims have been bled
Red velvet lines the black box.
Bela Lugosi's dead
Bela Lugosi's dead
Undead, undead, undead"

Bauhaus, "Bela Lugosi's Dead"

"Vampires are the reflection of the evil that we all hold in our hearts. That's why people believe in vampires."

Jacques Sirgent

Contents

Reader, FEAR NOT, I Bring You No Harm...

AFTER ALL THE CENTURIES I'VE WALKED THIS EARTH, even if my desire for fresh blood hasn't yet dried up, I've grown tired of hunting mortals. Life seems to repeat itself relentlessly: the future has started to taste of endless re-beginnings. When you live too long, the past starts to look rosier than the present... That's why, during a long night of restlessness, this wonderful idea began to germinate within me: to cast my mind even further back in time than my own birth. To dig up the story of my ancestors and try to understand how it all began.

I had to go back a long way, since we vampires have been with you, dear humans, for your entire history. Whether in the form of a vengeful goddess, the bloodthirsty undead, or, finally, a monster more refined—we've been by your side for thousands of years. There we are in your shadow, perched on your shoulder since the very beginnings of humanity, unseen reflections of your ancestral fears and repressed desires.

Just like you invented the devil, it is you who created us and, in telling our story, I'll also be telling yours.

Are you tempted?

Vampires AROUND the world

The *nukekubi*
Japan

Japanese folklore is home to many spirits and monsters grouped together as *yokai*. In this vast pantheon, the *nukekubi* is a vampiric creature who, by day, takes on the appearance of a woman. At night, her head detaches from her body to go out and bite living beings. It's then, when she's going about her bloody business, that you can destroy a *nukekubi*. There also exists a variation on this type: the *rokorukubi*, whose neck can stretch to an infinite length.

The *jiangshi*
China

The *jiangshi* or "stiff corpse" is half zombie, half vampire, and attacks mortals to suck their life force. Dressed in the attire of a mandarin or court official, they can only move by making little leaps, arms extended and holding their clawed hands out in front of them.

The *adze*
Togo and Ghana

In Ewe folkore, the *adze* is a vampire that takes the form of a harmless insect, most often a firefly, to get under bedroom doors and drink your blood while you sleep. They're particularly keen on the blood of children. There's no way of protecting yourself from an *adze*, other than to kill it before it turns back into human form. Even then, watch out—*adzes* can take control of humans with their mind.

The *soucouyant*
The Caribbean

During the day, the *soucouyant* looks like an old lady, but come nightfall she transforms into a ball of fire. This ball gets into houses through keyholes and cracks, to suck people's blood while they sleep. When they wake up, these victims become *soucouyants* themselves.

The *yara-ma-yha-who*
Australia

According to Aboriginal myth, the *yara-ma-yha-who* is a little red creature with an enormous head and a big, toothless mouth. They hide in fig trees waiting for an unsuspecting passerby whose blood they can suck with the suckers on their hands and feet. It's said that they can swallow their victims whole before spitting them out in one piece, repeating the process again and again until the victim has also turned into a *yara-ma-yha-who*.

The *manananggal*
Philippines

Described as looking like a beautiful old woman, the *manananggal* leaves its legs behind at night to fly through the air on wings that resemble a bat's. This vampire mostly targets pregnant women. To destroy a *manananggal*, they say you need to sprinkle salt, garlic, and ash on the abandoned legs. Unable to find its other half, the winged torso will roam until the first light of morning, which is deadly to the *manananggal*.

The *tlahuelpuchi*
Mexico

Half-vampire, half-witch, the *tlahuelpuchi* transforms herself into an animal so she can get into homes. In animal form, her telltale feature is a halo of light. Legend has it that *tlahuelphuchis* live a peaceful life until puberty, when they discover both their powers and their thirst for blood. From then on, they try to satisfy their need each nightfall, when they prey in particular on newborn babies.

Antiquity & THE ORIGINS of Thirst

BLOOD, THE VAMPIRE'S LIFE SOURCE, has an important place in most historical cultures. From China through pre-Columbian America via Mesopotamia and ancient Greece, vampires are feared and glorified in equal measure, and find themselves at the heart of important community rituals. Throughout the ancient world, the imagination is filled with creatures thirsty for blood. Antiquity was a time of myths, with pantheons of bloodthirsty goddesses and hordes of demons, seizing the souls of the dead in order to torment the living. These creatures embody a fear that has haunted humanity since the dawn of time: the fear of the return of the dead.

In ancient times, the undead weren't flesh and blood—their thirst for blood was restricted to the world of the gods. But this history is important for me in tracing where I came from. It reveals how Lamia, Sekhmet, and Lamashtu are distant ancestors of mine. Meanwhile, in ancient Greece, the connection drawn between blood and the underworld gets to the very essence of the vampire.

The reign OF BLOODTHIRSTY goddesses

WHEN VAMPIRES first achieved their fame through fiction, in literature, and then in cinema, they were given an exclusively masculine form. Being myself a creature of the night, I am proof—if not exactly *living* proof—that this was mistaken. In fact, the bloodthirsty creatures of antiquity had one thing in common: they all took the form of powerful goddesses.

Among these ancient goddesses are Lilith and Lamashtu. Demons of Mesopotamian mythology, they revel in the flesh and blood of men, with a particular taste for children and newborns. It's said that Lamashtu causes miscarriages and terrible nightmares. Amulets and bronze shields from the neo-Assyrian era (around the 8th century BCE) represent her as having a lion's head and claws instead of feet. Along with a taste for blood, the lion's head is a feature she shares with the Egyptian goddess Sekhmet, who is said to have escaped the control of her father—the god Ra—to the point where he had to trick her into drinking a potion that looked like blood so as to satisfy her thirst and stop her from destroying all of humankind.

But the Ancient Greeks were not to be outdone: theirs was the playground of Lamia and Empusa. Lamia, tearing children from their parents, would devour them and drink their blood, while Empusa, sent by the goddess Hecate, fed on the blood of the young as they slept. In the course of time, these figures would be written about as mothers of the lamias—mythological monsters half woman, half snake—and empusas—demons with one leg made of copper and the other that of a donkey.

Lamia

THEY SAY LAMIA STARTED OUT AS A QUEEN renowned for her beauty—so much so that the god Zeus seduced her. Several children were born from their love. But Zeus's wife Hera was eaten up with jealousy. According to some versions of the tale, she took her revenge in the cruellest possible way. Using her magic, she sent Lamia into a trance of murderous madness, causing her to kill her own children. When poor Lamia awoke from the terrible charm, her horror and grief at what she had done toppled her into a permanent state of derangement. Her pain disfigured both her body and face, transforming her into a bloodthirsty monster. They say she was particularly threatening to children and newborns. From her story, we get the legend of the lamias, demons with the appearance of beautiful young women, attracting men only to devour them...

Revenants OF THE ancient world

IN ANTIQUITY, it was a common belief that the souls of the dead could survive and transform into demonic spirits, known as revenants, if they weren't given proper burials, or if they died in particular circumstances. The Roman Empire had figures called *lemures* or *larvae*: this is what they called the souls of those who had died violent or tragic deaths but, not having been properly laid to rest, continued to haunt the homes of the living. There was a festival in their name, the Lemuralia, during which people performed rituals to appease the *lemures* and keep them at bay.

In Mesopotamia, it was believed that the souls of the unburied dead could come back in the form of the *edimmu*—a vengeful spirit who causes illness and possesses the bodies of the living, driving them to crime. Much like the Roman *lemures*, the *edimmu* is more of a phantom than a vampire, since it has neither a body nor a thirst for blood. There's one detail, though, that has always caught my attention, so strongly does it resonate with the kind of being I am: the *edimmu* is said to return to suck the life from the living as they sleep.

Finally, it's to Hindu tradition that I managed to trace the roots of the revenant with a body. That's in the figure of the *vetala*, another consequence of death without a funeral whose corpse, possessed by an evil spirit, wanders cemeteries, tricking and occasionally attacking the living.

Philinnion, living dead of antiquity

IN THE 2ND CENTURY CE, Phlegon of Tralles, a favorite of the Roman Emperor Hadrian, published his *Book of Marvels*, a collection of ghost stories and tales of all kinds of supernatural beings. Among these stories, he gave us the tragic tale of Philinnion and Machates, the oldest fantasy story ever told. It evokes the figure of a flesh-and-blood spirit, the earliest of my precursors of this nature to walk among mortals. In the story, the young Machates goes to live with a couple whose daughter, Philinnion, has just died. On his first night there, a woman shows up at the young man's room to try to seduce him into spending the night with her. Unbeknownst to Machates, that woman is Philinnion returned from the dead. Several nights pass this way, and the woman always disappears before dawn... until the day when her parents finally see her and she dies once again, this time for eternity, plunging her loved ones into infinite sadness and Machates into a despair so intense that he ends his own life. Philinnion's tomb is then opened, only to show there is nothing inside. Without strictly being a vampire tale, this early text laid the groundwork for numerous stories in which a femme fatale conceals her monstrosity beneath a seductive disguise so as to harm a young man by preying on his naivety.

"IT WAS DECIDED THAT WE SHOULD GO TO HER TOMB, OPEN IT AND SEE IF THE BODY WAS STILL IN ITS COFFIN OR IF WE WOULD FIND IT EMPTY. HALF A YEAR HAD PASSED SINCE THE YOUNG GIRL'S DEATH. [...] WHERE PHILINNION HAD BEEN LAID TO REST, WE FOUND ONLY THE IRON RING WHICH BELONGED TO OUR GUEST, AND THE GILDED WINE CUP—OBJECTS SHE HAD TAKEN FROM HIM ON HIS FIRST DAY WITH US."

Phlegon of Tralles, *Book of Marvels* (2nd century)

Blood, ELIXIR of the gods

"BLOOD IS LIFE," or so repeats Renfield, possessed by Bram Stoker's Dracula, over and over. Vital, animating fluid, the sight of it being poured sparks a mixture of terror and fascination—the reason it has always been a substance of choice for sacred rituals. For some Mesoamerican civilizations, most notably the Aztecs, blood was *chalcihuitl*, "precious water," offered to the gods in human sacrifices to nourish them and ensure the balance of the cosmos. In Shang dynasty China, blood was shed to win wars and bring on rain in times of drought. In ancient Rome, the doctor Celsus, in his treatise *De Medicina* ("On Medicine"), writes of how the blood of gladiators who died in the arena was used as a cure for epilepsy, which at the time was thought to be an illness sent by the gods.

However, it's in Greece that blood is explicitly linked to the world of the dead. The Ancient Greeks sacrificed animals to fearsome Hades, god of the underworld, as well as to those who lived in his kingdom. Blood was also used as a way of communicating with the dead. In a famous scene from Homer's epic poem, the *Odyssey*, Odysseus sacrifices a ram to the kingdom of the dead to bring them back to talk with him.

Blood has always played a part in sacred rituals aimed at winning favors from the gods by satisfying their thirst. With the birth of Judaism, one of the first religions to worship only one god, it also became an object of prohibition: since God is the sole master of life, and blood is life, it belongs to God and God alone. For that reason, it's reserved for the altar, and must never be drunk. This dietary rule aside, blood also has connotations of impurity, particularly for women, whose menstrual blood was considered impure in some ancient Hebrew texts, with rituals for cleansing baths to restore the woman's purity. With the ancient seeds of my family thus sown, Christianity and folklore became a perfect breeding ground for the legend of the vampire to grow and flourish over the centuries.

Lilith the accursed

IN HEBREW TRADITION, Lilith was the first wife of Adam, the first man. Fashioned from clay just like him, rather than made from his rib like Eve, she embodies a different kind of femininity—a free and independent one. Driven out of paradise without having eaten the forbidden fruit, as Adam and Eve did, Lilith remains immortal. It's possible that her name comes from the Mesopotamian goddess Lilith, a formidable demon who refused to take a husband, and who fed on the blood of newborns as they slept. People even made talismans to protect little infants in their cribs. The story varies according to time and tradition, but there is always the connection to blood. The Hebrew scriptures are very clear, though, when they give the supreme prohibition: "You shall not eat the blood of any creature, for the life of every creature is its blood." (Leviticus, XVII, 10–14). That's why bloodthirsty Lilith is cursed among all women.

Strigoi, the first Slavic vampires

SLAVIC MYTHOLOGY is also full of evil demons. Among those who aren't yet called "vampires" are the *strigoi*. Their legend goes back to the Dacians, who occupied Eastern Europe in the 1st century CE. The *strigoi* are living dead. At night, they come out of their tombs to torment the living. These are cursed souls, prevented from resting in peace because of their crimes when living. Their legend and their name derives, perhaps, from the Greco-Roman *strix*—sometimes a witch, sometimes a winged, blood-sucking monster, prowling around cemeteries. In this period, there are already myths telling that *strigoi* have the power to change into wolves, dogs, or night owls...

The MIDDLE AGES, When Revenants Take Shape

OVER THE CENTURIES, the reign of bloodthirsty gods slowly died out, taken over in Europe by a Christianity that recognized only one god, and which set out to make pagan superstition fade from memory. But you can't snuff out the fear of death so easily, nor can you banish fear of the dark.

The first accounts we have of attacks of "reanimated corpses" (the name for the living dead, risen from their tombs to torment the living) dates to the 11th century. No longer is there talk of phantoms or spirits—only bodies brought back to life by cursed souls, stripped of the right to rest in peace on account of their sinful lives.

A picture of my species is now beginning to take shape, and we're starting to see the threads that link it to Christianity. In Western Europe, Christianity popularized the idea of a blessed afterlife where pure souls could live forever as a reward for their good behavior. Without the idea of a "pure" soul, we wouldn't have the idea of a cursed one; and without cursed souls, no vampires. Would I even exist?

When the dead ARISE from the grave

A TEXT FROM THE EARLY 11TH CENTURY tells the story of a knight who, having died in exile from home, kept rising from the grave. Though he kept being buried again, his grave covered over with heavy rocks, he'd still manage to get out again the next day. The tale goes that he was reburied five times before he stayed in the ground. A century later, in England, another tale is told of a man who died from the plague, only to rise from the dead every night to torment his living neighbors. The corpse would call out their names until, in just a few days, they all caught the sickness too. In both stories, the man had been condemned in life for his terrible deeds. You don't deprive someone of a peaceful afterlife for nothing, after all...

Still, at this point in history, these undead have not yet taken to sucking blood. For medieval revenants, it was enough just to rise from the grave and kill the living from a distance. These "vampires" were still a long way from being given that name, and were nowhere near as scary to humans as they would go on to be. Then, you could simply cut off a corpse's head or burn it to stop it from attacking. There are very few medieval texts that bear witness to actions like these, but it seems that people in countries steeped in Scandinavian myths and Celtic legends were particularly prone to burning their dead.

The *draugar* of Norse sagas

IN NORSE MYTHOLOGY, the *draugr—draugar* in the plural—is a form of undead being whose traits foreshadow those of the vampire in a number of ways: they are revenants with bodies, filled with bad intentions and formidable strength, who prowl around houses by night without being able to cross the threshold, then return to their funeral mounds as soon as dawn breaks. To destroy one, you need to cut off its head while it's in the ground, then burn it, and dispose of the ashes in a stream. In some legends, the *draugr* has mystic powers, and its victims become able to transform themselves. It's the circumstances of death that determine whether a person will return as a *draugr*. Most often, they are men who have died in disgrace. Several Norse sagas from the Middle Ages describe the misdeeds of these dead who refuse to die. Among these is the Svarfdæla saga, part of which concerns the fate of Klaufi. The very same night that he was killed by his family, Klaufi reappeared as a *draugr* to his wife, who called her brothers to her aid. They managed to decapitate the revenant, but Klaufi continued to roam around the village, knocking on doors with his severed head, preying on men and their livestock. Each day he returned to his grave. In the end, they had to dig him out of the grave and burn him at the stake, putting his ashes in a leaden box that they threw into a hot spring. Never, after that, did they hear or speak of the *draugr*.

"THE BISHOP IN HIS WONDERMENT REPLIED, 'POWER, PERCHANCE, WAS GIVEN BY GOD TO THE EVIL ANGEL OF THAT WRETCH TO RENDER HIM RESTLESS IN HIS DEAD BODY. HOWEVER, DIG UP THE CORPSE, CUT THE NECK, AND BESPRINKLE THE BODY AND THE GRAVE WITH HOLY WATER, AND THEN REBURY IT.' ALTHOUGH THIS WAS DONE, NONETHELESS WERE THE SURVIVORS ASSAILED BY THE RESTLESS SPIRIT. ON A CERTAIN NIGHT, THEREFORE, WILLIAM [...] DREW HIS SWORD AND RUSHED OUT. AS THE DEMON FLED HE PURSUED IT TO THE VERY GRAVE, AND AS IT LAY THEREIN, HE CLAVE ITS HEAD TO THE NECK. FROM THAT HOUR CEASED THE PERSECUTION FROM THIS GHOSTLY WANDERER."

Walter Map, *De Nugis Curialium* (1193)

De Nugis Curialium is the only text written by Walter Map that remains to us.
It was a collection of anecdotes, including court gossip and a smattering of true history.
Map's style is satirical. Along with William of Newburgh, he told the first English stories we have of vampires.

Vampires AND EPIDEMICS

IF MY MEDIEVAL ANCESTORS weren't yet sucking their victims' blood, they had certainly already been crowned with a reputation for deadliness. Accused of bringing illness and vermin in their wake, they destined us to be associated forevermore with undesirable creatures—rats and parasites whose bite is feared by all, and which are burned in great heaps during pandemics.

The flourishing of vampire stories in the Middle Ages can be directly linked to epidemics, which sowed terror and despair all across Europe at that time. Most feared of all were plague epidemics, among them the Black Death, which wiped out a third of the European population in the middle of the 14th century. Death was everywhere, and faced with the scale of this disaster, survivors searched for an explanation—even a supernatural one would do—and were turning more than ever towards religion as a sole source of salvation. Without a doubt, it was during this century that rumors began to spread about dead people whose bodies had been discovered intact. The pace of burials was increasing, with mass graves having to be dug for plague victims, sometimes without funeral rites for lack of time. Gravediggers would sometimes find themselves nose to nose with recently buried corpses. The spectacle of death, however, takes a while to show itself. In the days that follow someone's passing, their hair continues to grow. The body swells, sometimes giving it the illusion of life, and as the person's lips start to retract, their teeth become extra prominent. Could it be that the first ever portrait of the vampire was painted by death itself?

"[…] FOR THE ATMOSPHERE, POISONED BY THE VAGARIES OF THIS FOUL CARCASS, FILLED EVERY HOUSE WITH DISEASE AND DEATH BY ITS PESTIFEROUS BREATH. ALREADY DID THE TOWN, WHICH BUT A SHORT TIME AGO WAS POPULOUS, APPEAR ALMOST DESERTED; WHILE THOSE OF ITS INHABITANTS WHO HAD ESCAPED DESTRUCTION MIGRATED TO OTHER PARTS OF THE COUNTRY, LEST THEY TOO SHOULD DIE […] WHEN THAT INFERNAL HELL-HOUND HAD THUS BEEN DESTROYED, THE PESTILENCE WHICH WAS RIFE AMONG THE PEOPLE CEASED, AS IF THE AIR, WHICH HAD BEEN CORRUPTED BY THE CONTAGIOUS MOTIONS OF THE DREADFUL CORPSE, WERE ALREADY PURIFIED BY THE FIRE WHICH HAD CONSUMED IT."

William of Newburgh, *Historia Regis Anglicarum* (1196)

Fear of the living dead

ALL OVER EUROPE, archaeologists have found evidence of burials we call "deviant," which demonstrate the medieval belief in the return of the dead, and most of all the fear it provoked. Death was seen as a transformation—you couldn't come back from it the same, so you had to make sure the dead stayed dead at all costs. Archaeologists have also found burnt shoes in tombs dating to the Roman Empire, a practice that seems to have been aimed at preventing any post-death wandering. Dug-up skeletons dating from the Middle Ages to the 17th century have been found with rocks jammed in their mouths, sickles under their chins, or even nailed to their tombs, belly to the ground. It seems there was a trend for facedown burials in the early 14th century—a time when devastating epidemics swept through medieval Europe. One of the most famous cases of a deviant burial took place in a plague hosptial in Venice in the 16th century, when a plague-ridden woman was buried with a brick in her mouth.

The Renaissance, A DANCE Led by the Devil

IN 1484, POPE INNOCENT VIII officially recognized the existence of demons and witchcraft. If stories of the living dead were viewed by the medieval Church as superstitions to be fought, in the Renaissance they were seen as the devil incarnate, showing the full force of his power. Demonologists say the living dead were enemy number one for the Catholic faith, and witches, who were accused of being their servants, were made to answer for their actions. For two centuries, under the banner of the Inquisition, Western Europe was ablaze with their pyres (humans can be just as monstrous as we vampires). In the wake of these persecutions, revenants were explained as the work of witchcraft, and were thought to prove the existence of the devil. Back then, however, they took the form of the werewolf, who came to take center stage. Stories of humans-turned-wolf traveled as far as Eastern Europe, tracing the outline of what humans would soon call "vampires."

Demonology AND VAMPIRIC phenomena

WRITTEN IN 1486, THE *MALLEUS MALEFICARUM* is a guide to prosecuting witches, which went hand-in-hand with the murderous witchhunts that took place over the next three centuries. In honoring this text, the Church underwent an ideological turn that would influence the whole Renaissance. From then on, there was no doubt that the devil was at work in the world's misfortunes. In those remote times, famines, plagues, every form of catastrophe was seen as a supernatural event. But in the eyes of the Church, the Evil One wasn't acting alone: witches were his servants, the living dead his allies. In every part of Catholic Europe this was the golden age of demonology, the "science of the devil," supported by the pope himself. Witchcraft, lycanthropy (the condition of being a werewolf), and the return of the dead were intimately tied to the devil, and even if vampires hadn't yet been named as such, demonologists were starting to offer theories as to their existence. Some agreed that we weren't exactly revenants, but demons who had taken possession of bodies, like the *vetala* of ancient India. Others still denied the existence of vampires, thinking of us as hallucinations—nightmares caused by the devil corrupting people's imaginations and souls.

Dance of the living dead

IN THE RENAISSANCE, THE LIVING DEAD of Catholic Europe were a devilish reversal of the resurrections depicted in the Bible. Unlike Lazarus, who in the Bible is brought back to life by Christ, and Christ himself, the kinds of dead brought back to life by a force other than God's can be distinguished by their disgusting appearance. They're a provocation of sorts—a haunting imitation of the divine immortality. They violate the ultimate laws of religion and nature, which declare that there is no return from death. We see this contrast in pictures of *danses macabres*, circles of the living moving hand in hand with the dead. In paintings that flourished at the start of the 15th century, dancing skeletons and corpses show a morbid joy that contrasts with the dignity and reflectiveness we see in traditional depictions of saints.

This is the ancestor of my brood: a rival resurrection, an antihuman who makes a mockery of the laws of God and nature and who, in his wake, brings death

The origins of the nightmare

SINCE ANCIENT TIMES, the nightmare has been associated with the idea of oppression. As for the word itself, the "mare" part comes from the Old English *mære*, which names a kind of demon, as do similar words in many European languages. Old stories of nightmares tell of how they were caused by demons, who, taking their place on the chest of a sleeping victim, would give them the horrible feeling of not being able to breathe.

Vampires AND WEREWOLVES

TODAY, VAMPIRES AND WEREWOLVES don't have much more in common than sharp teeth and a taste for blood. In distant times, however, the two creatures were closely linked. In Greece, for example, it was said that those mysterious revenants who weren't yet called vampires had been werewolves in their lifetimes. Or that werewolves were in fact dead people who had returned in animal form to feed on fresh blood. In some regions, notably Eastern Europe, they're called by the same name: the *vrykolakas.*

From the early 16th century, trials for lycanthropy were multiplying. An epidemic of werewolves seemed to be raging and, in the course of a century, no less than thirty thousand cases were tried in the courts. It's no coincidence that this was also the same time as the wave of trials for witchcraft was sweeping Europe, following the Church's official recognition of demonology.

Those who were convicted were most often men who had committed bestial crimes, or the ultimate sin: eating human flesh. Though there was never any evidence for their transformation into animals, the myth has stayed alive. As if cruelty could only be explained by putting it down to some monstrous part of a person, distinguishing the criminal from the rest of humankind...

Transcript from the trial of Jacques Roulet, the Angevin "werewolf," tried in 1598.

JUDGE: WHEN RUBBED WITH THIS OINTMENT DO YOU BECOME A WOLF?
JACQUES ROULET: NO; BUT FOR ALL THAT, I KILLED AND ATE THE CHILD CORNIER: I WAS A WOLF.
JUDGE: WERE YOU DRESSED AS A WOLF?
JACQUES ROULET: I WAS DRESSED AS I AM NOW. I HAD MY HANDS AND MY FACE BLOODY, BECAUSE I HAD BEEN EATING THE FLESH OF THE SAID CHILD.

The Gandillon family

In 16th-century France, the Jura region and its surroundings were the site of numerous lycanthropy trials. One of these involved a whole family: the Gandillons. It all started with the story of a boy attacked in the forest by a wolf whose paws bore a strange resemblance to hands. Rumors immediately spread around the village that the perpetrator was Perrenette Gandillon. She had been found covered in blood and brandishing the murder weapon—not claws or fangs, but a simple knife, which seemed to leave no doubt as to her guilt. The story didn't stop there though, and soon Pierre Gandillon, Perrenette's brother, also became a suspect. Accused of traveling across the country in the form of a wolf, and of practicing dark magic, he was arrested with his other sister Antoinette and her son Georges. The Gandillons eventually confessed that they owed their transformation to a special ointment given to them by the devil himself. They claimed that all they needed to do to become human again was to roll around in wet grass. Henry Boguet, the demonologist in charge of the trial, claimed in *An Examen of Witches* (1603) that the prisoners moved around on all fours and howled and growled in their cells. Charged with lycanthropy, the family was condemned to the stake in 1598.

Eastern EUROPE, Land of the Vampire

IN EASTERN EUROPEAN COUNTRIES, the figure of the revenant took on a strong personality very early in history. The 12th-century chronicle *The Tale of Bygone Years*, attributed to a monk named Nestor, includes the story of a Russian village beset by the living dead, hungry for fresh meat. While in Western Europe demonology is mostly concerned with witches and werewolves, a completely different story is written into the history of the East, far from the stakes of the Inquisition: the story of my vampire ancestors, who in Eastern Europe find the perfect setting for their nighttime excursions. During the very first glimmers of the Renaissance, the one they call "Dracula" was sowing terror and causing bloodshed in Wallachia. At the same time, people thought they heard the dead groaning in their tombs, busy devouring themselves, and feared that they would soon covet the blood of the living.

In the 17th century, a wave of vampirism seems to have descended on the countryside. Slowly but surely, the figure of the *upyr* comes into being, fed by local legends and the tales of werewolves brought by travelers from the West.

The shroud-MUNCHING dead

IN THE 14th CENTURY, the rhythm of daily life was practically set by epidemics. The dead were buried hastily in mass graves, and with these waves of death came rumors which spread across Prussia, Bohemia, and Silesia (now Germany, Poland, and Czechia). It was thought that some of the dead were eating through their shrouds, their clothes and finally their own flesh, so avidly that they could be heard groaning and chewing in their coffins "like pigs." From the grave, these living dead, who in Germany were called *nachzehrers*, were held responsible for killing their loved ones and starting more epidemics, never stopping until their meals had been finished and digested. These shroud-munchers were quick to become the subject of many tales and treatises, of which one was the notorious *Malleus Maleficarum*.

While at first contained to their tombs, *nachzehrers* grew more dangerous towards the end of the 16th century, particularly in Protestant countries like Germany. It was claimed that these undead creatures weren't content with their own shrouds, and had started leaving the grave to attack their own families and drink their blood. You would find them sated and stained with red when you opened up their coffins, and the only way to stop their terrible doings was to impale them on a sword or take a stake to their heart. In the land of the East, the vampire had truly come alive.

Outbreaks of hasty burials

When death takes too many of the living in one go, the pace of burials becomes frantic. Think, if you will, of the Black Death, which ravaged the whole of Europe and did away with 25 million people in just a few years. Panic, mingled with the fear of contagion, produced the inevitable result: some of the living were buried by mistake. It's hard to know for sure how many of the sick actually awoke to find themselves entombed, who devoured their own shrouds and sometimes even their own hands in the last hope of escaping the horrific fate that wanted them dead before their time. When, drawn in by the noise, people found the tombs of such people, it was generally too late. The terrible sight they were faced with—bodies smeared with blood, half-eaten shrouds between their teeth, was enough to terrify even the bravest of souls.

This fear would linger for a very long time, if it was extinguished at all. It wasn't until the 19th century that systems were put in place to allow those who were concerned about themselves to warn of their possible "resurrection," and medical treatises began to command that the dead were officially pronounced dead before they were buried.

The dark of night, blood, sickness, and now burial—is there any source of fear I can't embody for you, dear humans?

"What good are your magnificent funerals in the face of the despair of the one you have abandoned and forgotten as soon as the appearance of life left his body, and who will come to in the depths of his coffin to die there for real?"

Maximilien Kaufmann, *On the Appearance of Death and on Hasty Burial* (1851)

Vlad the Impaler (c.1448-1476)

TOWARDS THE END of the Middle Ages, a particularly cruel character reigned over Wallachia, a region of present-day Romania. Vlad III was *vovoide* (prince) of this small country. The Orthodox and Catholic region, caught in a vice between Christian Hungary and the Ottoman Empire of Muslim Turks, was a theater of deceitful alliances and bloody betrayals.

Vladislav III went by the name of Dracula or "son of the dragon," a diabolical surname taken by all his family following his father's allegiance to the notorious Order of the Dragon. It was said he took great pleasure in the massacres he ordered. He was even depicted seated in front of a veritable forest of impaled enemies, a form of torture used liberally in the region for executing captured enemies. It was this that gave him the name "the Impaler," or *Tepes* in Romanian. His reputation, and later his disgrace—he died in battle with the Turks and his head was brought to the Sultan on a stake—certainly contributed to how the myth of the vampire was constructed. The history of Vlad III was just one anecdote among many, until four centuries later, a certain Bram Stoker was inspired to create the vampire of all vampires: Count Dracula.

"One day, Dracula sent an announcement through the country that the elderly and sick, the poor and the infirm should come to him. And he gathered together a massive crowd of vagabonds and peasants, who waited to receive his charity. Then he ordered that they all come together in a big house, and commanded that they be served whatever food and drink they wanted. [...] Then Dracula himself came to pay them a visit, and said: [...] 'Would you like me to make it so that you no longer have a care in the world; that you want for nothing?' With that, he ordered that the house be set fire to, and all of them burned to death."

15th-century chronicle, quoted in Matei Cazacu, *The Story of Dracula in Central and Eastern Europe* (1988)

Elizabeth Báthory (1560-1614)

IN 1610, A DELEGATION was sent to Čachtice Castle (in present-day Slovakia), home of the countess Elizabeth Báthory. Worrying tales of disappearing girls had been spreading in the region, and rumors as to the involvement of the castle's mistress had got as far as the king of Hungary. A terrible sight awaited the king's envoys when they arrived. They reported having seen the bloodless corpse of a young girl, and a dozen servants dying in the basement with the awful smell of putrefaction filling the air. The countess was placed under house arrest, but her title allowed her to escape a disgraceful trial. But her alleged accomplices—her servants—did not receive the same favorable treatment. They were brought to justice and condemned to death. Witnesses had reported crimes that seemed beyond comprehension: for ten years, the countess had abused her status to subject young girls to countless atrocities, having her chambermaids hire them as servants. Báthory was condemned to be locked in the castle for the rest of her life. She died there in 1614. Over time, genuine history and popular mythology began to blend into each other. It started with tales that the countess bathed in the blood of her young victims, thinking this was an elixir of youth; that she went so far as to feast on them just to preserve her own beauty. Today, some historians believe Báthory was the victim of a conspiracy by other nobles eager to get their hands on her wealth. Left to ruin after the death of its mistress, the accursed castle, with its gothic keep and high crenelated walls, became the model for Bram Stoker when he imagined the residence of Dracula. It is thought that, several centuries after their lives, the writer brought together the diabolical countess and the prince of blood, Vlad III, in his fiction.

The faces OF THE VAMPIRE multiply

IN THE 17th CENTURY, in Central Europe and the Balkans, belief in vampires spread and took root via local folklore. *Strigoi, upyr, vârcolac, moroi...* though the local names and details varied, all of them described a creature with a body brought back from the dead who attacked living people and ultimately killed them. In the countryside, people got caught up in a real vampire hunt, which again coincided with great waves of epidemics—plague and cholera, which decimated populations in Eastern Europe. Suspected culprits were everywhere. The dead had their rest disturbed as it became a common practice to dig up their graves and burn their remains in attempts to destroy these unholy beings forever. How to explain the origins of my ancestors? For a long time, people have blamed the supposed ignorance and superstition of people in remote and mountainous regions, shut off from the intellectual progress of the Renaissance. But what about those countries in Western Europe which, in the very same century, were pitilessly burning those they suspected of being witches and werewolves? In those far-off times, science was still in its infancy, and it was easier for a society to find a scapegoat for things that went wrong than to question the powers that be. People found comfort in religion, which was what helped them to make sense of the terrible things that befell humanity. While the Catholic Church in the West made people fight demons with forced trials and burning at the stake, the Orthodox Church, which was the dominant one in the East, was more accepting of pagan beliefs. These were allowed to be expressed and circulated more widely, much like vampires themselves, who before long were a subject of interest even for the most powerful rulers in Western Europe.

"YOU, STRIGOI,
YOU, MOROI,
YOU, LION
YOU, CASTER OF SPELLS
[...]
GO
TO WHERE THE MAIDEN DOESN'T BRAID HER HAIR
WHERE THE AXE MAKES NO SOUND AS IT FALLS
WHERE THE PRIEST DOESN'T READ THE BOOK,
INSIDE THE DEER'S HOOF
IN THE DEPTHS OF THE SEA,
GO THERE,
STAY THERE,
LEAVE [NAME OF VICTIM] ALONE
PURE,
SHINING,
LIKE THE PUREST SILVER,
LIKE THAT WHICH FALLS FROM THE SKY,
JUST AS GOD LEFT IT ON EARTH"

Romanian exorcism recited to deliver a human victim from a vampire, recounted by Adrien Cremene.

A gallery of Eastern European vampires

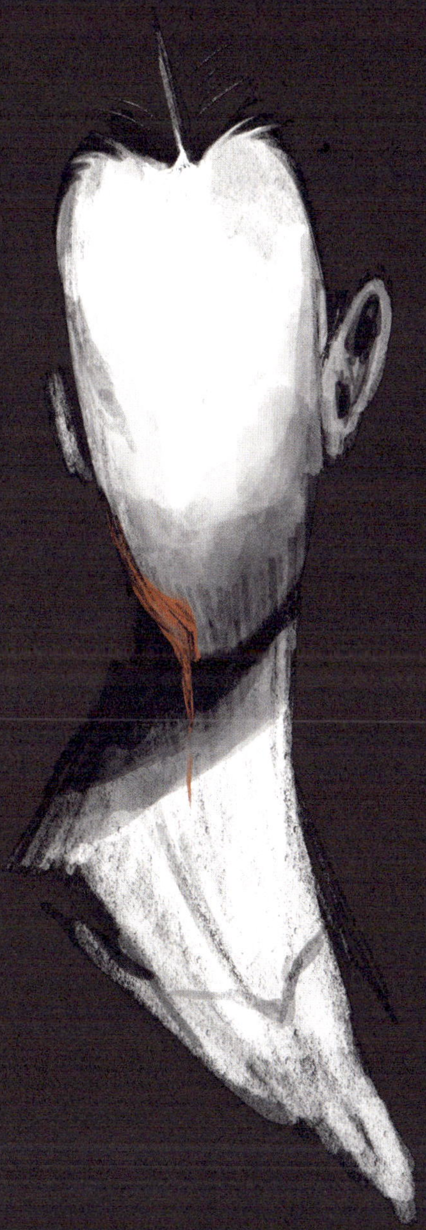

VRYKOLAKAS OR VORVOLAKAS

Greece, Serbia. These two similar names both describe a terrible revenant, whose body is found in its tomb completely intact and drenched in fresh blood. They can never be completely destroyed until they have been burned to ashes.

VOURDALAK

Bosnia, Dalmatia, Hungary, Russia, Serbia. A werewolf vampire who only attacks family and close friends. Described by Aleksey Konstantinovich Tolstoy in his novella, *The Family of the Vourdalak* (1884).

UPYR

Poland, Russia, Ukraine. A revenant brought to life by an evil spirit. Its name would have come from the Serbian *piriti*, which means "to swell." Over time, up until the 14th century, the terms *upyr* and vampire were both used to describe the same thing, until vampire came to dominate.

OBOUR

Bulgaria. A murdered person who, in the nine days following their death, wanders the night in the form of a shadow. After forty days, the *obour* regains possession of its corpse, and sets about terrorizing people and killing animals to drink their blood and keep on living.

STRIGOI

Romania. Generic name for the vampire. This one also exists in female form as a *striga*. Legend tells that if a cat or a dog passed over the body of a dead person, this would turn them into a *strigoi*.

NOSFERAT

Romania. Another word for vampire, the origin of this name is disputed—it may be a bad transcription of the word "necurat," which means "dirty" and is a word for an evil spirit. Another theory suggests that it comes from the Greek "nosophoros"—that which brings illness.

MOROI

Romania. Refers either to a child who died before baptism, or one whose parents were both vampires. The moroi rises from its tomb in the night to feed on the blood of the living, and is able to turn into a dog, a cat, a toad, a spider, or any number of creatures.

The Enlightenment PARADOX: the Vampire is Born

THE 18th CENTURY WAS A THEATER for the triumph of reason. It's known as the Age of Enlightenment, referring to the bright lights of knowledge, which are thought to have then lit up even the darkest corners of the world—the places where ignorance, the mother of all superstitions, hides in the shadows. Nevertheless, it is precisely in this period when the vampire becomes an obsession like no other. My ancestors wove their way from their native East to the most enlightened parts of Western Europe. The Church, which had only just put an end to its witch trials, began to turn its attention to a different target of divine justice. Local rumors began to morph into witness statement in trials ruled over by the highest authorities. Myths about the vampire from over the centuries began to fuse together and soon became set in stone: vampires were revenants with human bodies, which emerged from their tombs to suck victims' blood. There's still no mention at this point of sharpened teeth or a bewitching gaze—the vampire of folklore is simply a figure of the living dead, engorged with blood, unaware of his status, and not particularly seductive. It now becomes the mission of scientists and philosophers to destroy this monstrous being using the tools of rational thinking.

The vampire is BAPTIZED

IN CENTRAL EUROPE, the vampire craze continues to spread. Panic is so rife among the people that official inquisitions start being ordered in the highest places to try to shed light on the situation. These investigations resulted in many reports, one of which, published on July 21st, 1725, tells of a man named Peter Plogojowitz. This peasant from the village of Kisilova in Serbia was accused of having killed nine people after his own death. Each of the victims had claimed in their dying moments to have seen their former neighbor. When Plogojowitz's grave was dug up, there was his body, intact and bloated with blood. It's in this report that the vampire is first given a name. Several years later, another report, the *Visum et Repertum* ("Seen and Discovered") written by the doctor Johann Flückinger, records the case of Arnold Paole. It was said that this recently deceased man was terrorizing villagers and responsible for their deaths. Between these two cases, recorded in meticulous detail by scientists and men of the Church, the idea was spread that these villains were infiltrating Western Europe, with France at its epicenter. On March 3rd, 1732, an extract from Flückinger's report was translated and published in France by the well-known journal *Le Glaneur*. It was then that the word *vampyre* first appeared in French, followed by the English "vampire" in London newspapers. In 1738, the case of Arnold Paole was mentioned by the writer Jean-Baptiste de Boyer, Marquis d'Argens. The press immediately jumped on it, and news of the vampire spread like wildfire. And that's how, born in the shadows of Slavic villages, my ancestors made their sensational entrance into the gilded halls of Enlightenment Europe.

"In one Hungarian township [...] the people [...] believed that some of the dead, whom they called 'vampires,' were sucking the blood of the living such that they (the living) were visibly exhausted, while the corpses meanwhile were filled with so much blood that it leaked from their very pores."

Extract from *Le Glaneur* (1732)

The case of Arnold Paole

"Having heard from several sources that in the village of Medwegya in Serbia, so-called 'vampires' were killing a large number of people and sucking their blood, I have been commissioned by Her Majesty to throw some light on this question." So begins the report of military surgeon Johann Flückinger on the alleged vampire epidemic of 1727 to 1732, which began with four suspicious deaths that took place shortly after the death of one Arnold Paole. The decision was taken to dig up this man, and what the villagers found left them horrified, and more convinced than ever that he was indeed a vampire. He was found "perfectly preserved. His flesh had not decomposed, his eyes were filled with fresh blood, which also flowed from his ears and nose, soiling his shirt and funeral shroud." The vampire was burned, but not before the villagers drove a stake through his heart and chopped off his head. The same treatment was given to the remains of Paole's victims. Nevertheless, despite these measures, death continued to rain down, and many of the people whose bodies were exhumed were found to have the same vampire-like characteristics. These people were also declared vampires by Flückinger's military commission. Far from offering rational explanations for these disturbing events, the surgeon and other authorities were siding with popular opinion. It was established that Paole, vampire zero, had also sucked the blood of some animals, which were then eaten by the villagers, meaning that they became vampires too. To try and stem the epidemic, the dead were dug up en masse. Their remains were then burned to ashes and scattered in the river.

Dom Augustin CALMET and the quest for truth

TOWARDS THE MID-CENTURY, Dom Augustin Calmet, a well-read clergyman, decided to look further into the waves of official reports that were coming out of Germany and countries in the East. In 1746, he published what remains to this day the official reference work on vampires in the 18th century: *Dissertations on the appearance of angels, demons and spirits, and the ghosts and vampires of Hungary, Bohemia, Moravia, and Silesia.*

In this work of over a thousand pages, the clergyman takes it upon himself to compile every case of demonic apparition reported in the 17th and 18th centuries, and subjects them to his own theological analysis. For Calmet, these stories were too great a threat to the religious belief in life after death to simply be swept aside. Yet the Bible itself was full of demonic apparitions. How to explain the truth of those while refusing to pay attention to the people's claims to be witnessing demons in the present?

Calmet's position was clear: "If the return of vampires is real, it must be proven, and if it false, it is in the utmost interests of the Church to disabuse those who believe it to be true." Dom Calmet then set about documenting dozens of cases, taken from trial reports and letters sent to him by witnesses. His research went all the way back to the ancient story of Phlegon of Tralles and the beautiful Philinnion; he looked into the existence of lamias, examining histories from every possible country. While his inquiry gave a kind of legitimacy to the vampire question, in the end it was his opinion that it was all nothing but an illusion. Mistreatment of the remains of suspected vampires, depriving them of their eternal rest, was to be severely punished from then on.

The pope's letter to the archbishop

IN 1756, IN A LETTER TO AN ARCHBISHOP who had asked him to respond to the existence of vampires in Poland, Pope Benedict XIV urged him to reject this idea. For the pope, this was a mere superstition, and in the letter he accused local priests of feeding this rumor for their own profit. Going on a report given by Gérard Van Swieten, chief physician to Maria Theresa, Holy Roman Empress, which had led to a decree banning anti-vampire activities in the Empire, the pope made absolutely clear the Catholic Church's position on the matter:

"It would seem to be Poland's special privilege, this right to wander around after death. Here, I can assure you, our dead are as peaceful as they are silent. [...] It falls to you, Archbishop, to put a stop to these superstitions. You'll find, if you follow them to their source, that there are priests giving weight to them so that naturally gullible people will pay them for exorcisms and masses. I command you immediately cast out, without exception, those who you find to be capable of such an abuse of power. And I beg that you assure yourself that only the living are at fault in this affair."

Voltaire and the vampire

THE FRENCH WRITER VOLTAIRE, when he dedicated an entry to the vampire in his *Philosophical Dictionary* (1764), intended to condemn the vampire frenzy that was shaking the entire era. The philosopher pointed a finger at the Church for breeding superstition, and in particular Dom Calmet, who "treated vampires in the same way as he treated the Old and New Testaments—faithfully reporting everything that was put in front of him." A surefooted opponent of the Church, Voltaire wasn't going to forgive that clergyman for taking the issue seriously. If he himself was bringing up the figure of the vampire, it was only to transform it into a social metaphor, one that quickly became popular among revolutionaries: the only vampires to believe in were "businessmen, who were sucking the blood of the people in plain sight."

Vampirism IN THE LIGHT of science and reason

PHILOSOPHERS AND INTELLECTUALS of the Enlightenment were scornful of those they saw as giving credibility to the worst superstitions. They set about to debunk the testimonies of these contemporaries by trying to give rational explanations for all the various things they reported. While men of the Church were anxious on behalf of God's word, these philosophers and doctors were above all concerned with ridding vampire stories of any trace of the supernatural. In particular, there was the *Medical Report on Vampires* written by the physician Gérard Van Swieten, who went back over many accounts of vampires to try and give them scientific and medical explanations. Genetic mutations, misunderstandings of the different stages of bodily decomposition after death, drug use, fragile mental states: these rational theories all came together and were marked by a certain contempt for overactive imaginations and tastes for the macabre. Reports of vampires were condemned as the result of nothing more than the ignorance of credulous peasants.

In the final decades of the 18th century, belief began to fade; the Enlightenment won out. The vampire had earned its name, but would no longer be a popular phenomenon… at least, we have learned to hide ourselves, in the dark recesses of fiction.

"IT IS ALL TOO EASY FOR SOME PEOPLE TO IMAGINE THEY ARE BEING SUCKED BY VAMPIRES, AND FOR THE FEAR THIS INSTILS IN THEM TO CAUSE SO MUCH INNER TURMOIL THAT IT SUCKS THEM OF ALL LIFE."

Marquis d'Argens, *Jewish Letters* (1736)

Vampirism put to the medical test

THE PHENOMENON OF SOME CORPSES STAYING INTACT and not others found a scientific explanation in 18th-century medicine. At the same time, parallels were being drawn between the traits of vampires and the symptoms of certain illnesses. Rabies, which is transmitted though animal bites, causes hallucinations, and can make the infected person behave aggressively to the point where they might even bite others. Tuberculosis, which is highly contagious, can kill an entire family in a short space of time, but not without first causing paleness, hypersensitivity to light, and the coughing up of blood. Finally, porphyria, a genetic blood disease, is not dissimilar to some of the things that afflict us vampires: the skin of those affected burns when exposed to the sun, their teeth, and nails take on reddish color, their gums rot away, making their teeth appear very long, and their hair grows at an alarming rate. Some people with this illness are also allergic to allicin, a compound found mainly in... garlic.

The Vampire TRANSFORMS

"THANKS TO THE INSIGHTS OF PHILOSOPHY, vampires are no longer in fashion." With this brief entry in his *Infernal Dictionary* of 1818, Jacques Auguste Simon Collin de Plancy sounded the death knell of superstitions from Eastern Europe. But patience! Legends can only really unfold when we pretend to have forgotten them... And what is Enlightenment reason compared to thirst for darkness buried in the depths of your immortal souls? So what if the half-baked vampire of rural myth no longer interests an "enlightened" society? The nightmare will inevitably change its shape. After all, transformation is what we vampires do best.

The 19th century was a time of great passion—a cradle of feeling from the most unbridled Romanticism to the darkest fantasies. Can it be any coincidence that only a year after the *Infernal Dictionary* was published, John Polidori published his novel *The Vampyre*? Poets and writers were the first to give new flesh to the bones of my brood. So it was that we morphed into passionate beings, aristocrats, and libertines, who dealt to our victims a death cloaked in pleasure. And when, at the end of the century, Bram Stoker incorporated Transylvanian legends into his fiction, the fusion was complete. The myth was born.

A triumph OF INK AND BLOOD

FROM THE END OF THE 18th CENTURY, literature revels in the figure of the vampire. In Germany, seat of Romanticism, Heinrich Ossenfelder wrote *Der Vampir* in 1746, and the renowned Johann Wolfgang von Goethe published *The Bride of Corinth* in 1797. With these two poems a distinctly romantic relationship was being established between the vampire and their victim, each work skilfully uniting death and passion. But it's in the 19th century that literature really takes hold of the theme, starting with *The Vampyre*, written in 1819 by John Polidori. At the same writing workshop where Mary Shelley's *Frankenstein* was born, the young doctor helped to sketch out one of the founding vampires of literary mythology. This was his vengeance on his employer, the English Romantic poet Lord Byron, whom Polidori hated with all his heart. The vampire in question, Lord Ruthven, a wily and privileged seductor, does indeed have a strong resemblance to the famous writer... The story of *The Vampyre* was adapted for theater, and became a huge success in Great Britain. The island of Britain was a fertile breeding ground at the time for myths and legends, incubating a great deal of fantastical literature. In the corseted, puritan society of the Victorian era, the desire for freedom burrowed deep in the cultural imagination. "Penny Dreadfuls" were all the rage—cheap magazines filled with gothic tales of revenants and monsters. In France, Théophile Gautier published *La Morte Amoureuse* in 1836, and Alexandre Dumas wrote a play called *Le Vampire* in 1851. Inspired by Elizabeth Báthory, Irish author Sheridan Le Fanu imagined Carmilla—*femme fatale* in the eyes of many—in his 1872 novella of the same name. Little by little, literature had given us vampires an unparalleled renown. By the end of the century, we would have risen to the status of modern myth with the publication of Bram Stoker's *Dracula*.

Romantic heroes and femmes fatales

THE ROMANTIC IMAGINATION transformed the brutal revenant of the Eastern European countryside in both appearance and social status. Now an aristocratic figure—a *femme fatale* or a dangerous "dandy"—the vampire had become a thinking being, conscious of their own condition, who plays on the naivety of their prey to satisfy their thirst for blood. The Romantics projected on this creature several ideas that were close to their hearts: immortality and the loneliness it brings, and the wandering of cursed souls, as alluring as they are monstrous, forced by their nature to be relegated to the margins, misunderstood by mortals. Not just a predator, the vampire now stood at the center of an existential drama, prisoner of a condition they did not choose, who must deal with an immortality from which they can never be saved. The vampire's darkness acquires a certain nuance—they are said to be capable of feeling, as exemplified by Polidori, whose novel tells "the story of a vampire who spent many years in the company of his parents and dearest friends, only to be forced to prolong his existence, arising for several months a year to devour someone he loves."

Victorian England shivers with delight

IN 1837, THE ASCENSION OF QUEEN VICTORIA to the throne of the United Kingdom saw society imprisoned in a straitjacket of values, both rigid and austere. The horror genre became a way of subverting this stifling morality—a genre in which we vampires embody the spirit of transgression, scandal, and sacrilege. Our bite becomes a kiss, our thirst for blood transforms into desire. Writers dress up their texts by skilfully melding the feelings of terror and desire. To you mortals, we become synonymous with a dangerous passion. Polidori's Lord Ruthven, for example, is a rogue dandy who takes pleasure in seducing the purest souls before dragging them to their death, while Le Fanu's mysterious Carmilla entertains a passion for the young Laura who, captivated by the vampire, ends up succumbing.

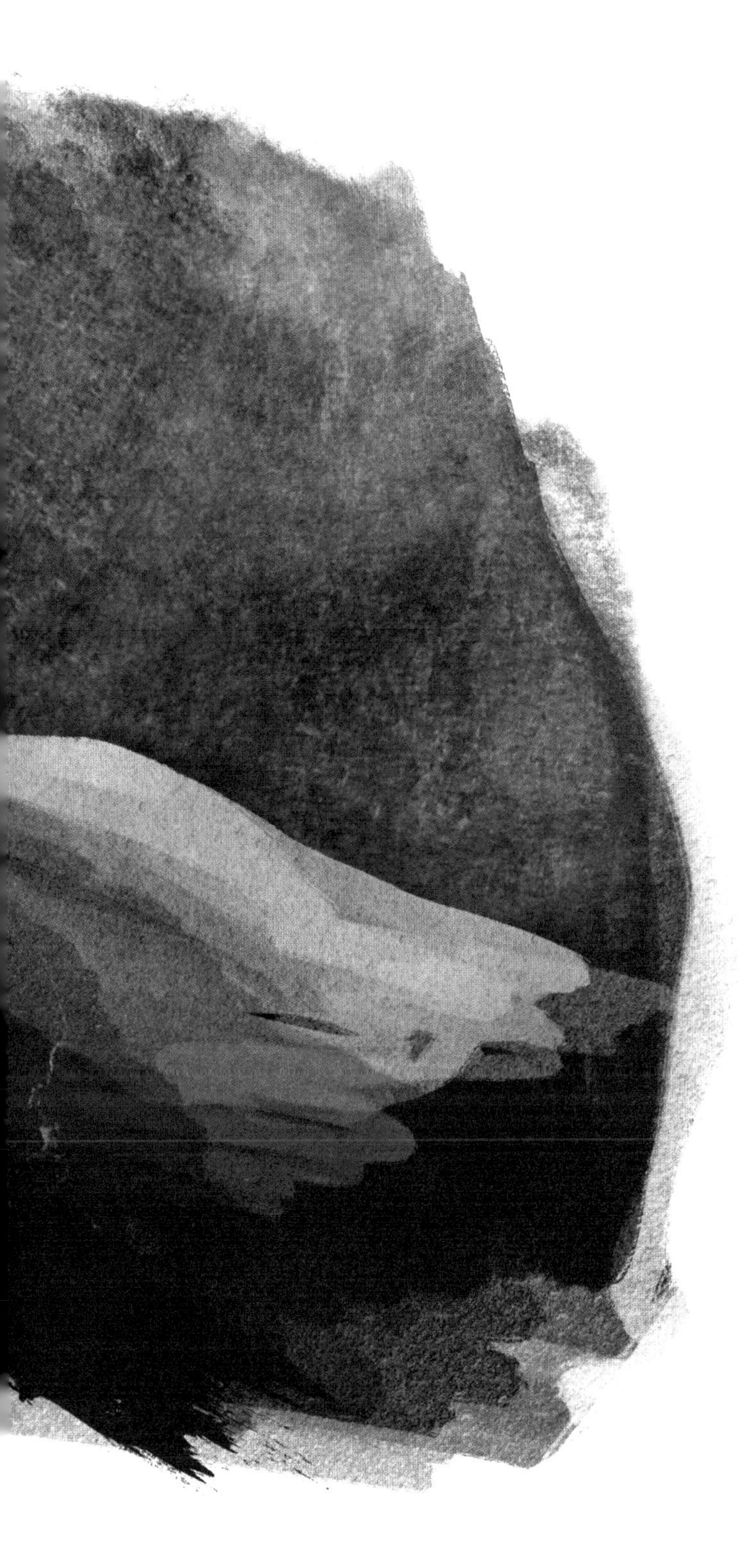

"She used to place her pretty arms about my neck, draw me to her, and laying her cheek to mine, murmur with her lips near my ear, 'Dearest, your little heart is wounded; think me not cruel because I obey the irresistible law of my strength and weakness; if your dear heart is wounded, my wild heart bleeds with yours. In the rapture of my enormous humiliation I live in your warm life, and you shall die—die, sweetly die—into mine. I cannot help it; as I draw near to you, you, in your turn, will draw near to others, and learn the rapture of that cruelty, which yet is love; so, for a while, seek to know no more of me and mine, but trust me with all your loving spirit.'"

Sheridan Le Fanu, *Carmilla* (1872)

Dracula
THE MODERN MYTH

BRAM STOKER wasn't always a writer. At first, he was a theater manager. Fascinated by the occult and the fantastical stories around it, he decided to write one of his own, and would later say he'd been inspired by a nightmare. A real perfectionist, he threw himself into studying the original Romanian myth. But it was Arminius Vámbéry, a Hungarian professor of Turkish languages, who redirected Stoker's writing towards the one he called the Vampire Count. As soon as the professor told him about Vlad Tepes, Stoker deepened his research and one day stumbled on a footnote: *dracul*, in Romanian, had come to mean "devil." It was thus that the Vampire Count became Dracula. The novel starts with the journey of Jonathan Harker, a young English notary clerk charged with traveling to Transylvania to the home of the mysterious Count Dracula, who is hoping to buy a property in England. The young man very quickly realizes that the count isn't all he seems: he has no reflection, never appears in the light of day, and is stirred by the sight of blood. When one day he sees him in his coffin, Jonathan understands that his host is a vampire... who has taken him prisoner. On his return to London, he and his wife Mina Harker discover that his former jailer is sowing death and desolation there. With the help of Professor Abraham Van Helsing, will they manage to free themselves from the vampire's grip and destroy him?

With his plot straddling London and the count's Transylvanian castle, Bram Stoker creates a perfect synthesis between the original vampire myth, from which he draws important characteristics, and the ambivalent figure of the vampire that emerges in the 19th century. The count is at once bestial and aristocratic; monstrous and intriguing. Even Mina Harker pities him, sympathetic to the weight of his curse. *Dracula* found immediate success, with the poet and playwright Oscar Wilde going so far as to declare it "the most beautiful novel of the century." Thus the modern vampire was born, and continued to flourish in the following century thanks to an art form that has never stopped drawing inspiration from us: cinema.

Bram Stoker and Marie Nizet

THE FATHER OF DRACULA, BRAM STOKER, willingly disclosed the sources of inspiration that helped him write his famous novel. But there was one inspiration he never mentioned in his lifetime: *Captain Vampire*. Yet this novel, written in 1879 by a young Belgian author named Marie Nizet, foreshadowed many of the features of *Dracula* that made it such a success. In it, two Romanian couples fall prey to a vampire, who is a prince and colonel in the Russian army. Twenty years before Bram Stoker, Marie Nizet was thus the first to set her vampire novel in Eastern Europe. Above all, the Irish author owes to *Captain Vampire* some of his own vampire's defining traits: he's an aristocratic outsider, come to conquer the land of the novel's protagonists, endowed with a terrifying strength despite his thin, pale face, and gifted a hypnotic power which he used to subdue his victims before feasting on their blood.

"THE POOR SOUL WHO HAS WROUGHT ALL THIS MISERY IS THE SADDEST CASE OF ALL. JUST THINK WHAT WILL BE HIS JOY WHEN HE, TOO, IS DESTROYED IN HIS WORSER PART THAT HIS BETTER PART MAY HAVE SPIRITUAL IMMORTALITY."

Bram Stoker, *Dracula* (1897)

The Mercy Brown case

WE HAVE REACHED THE USA at the end of the 19th century. A tuberculosis epidemic is wreaking havoc and destroying entire households, including that of the Brown family. The mother is the first to die, followed swiftly by the eldest daughter. After that, it's the turn of Mercy, who succumbs during a winter so cold that the ground freezes. Her body is kept in a crypt for several days before she is placed in a coffin. But the miseries of the Brown family don't stop there. The father is spared, but the health of his son, Edwin, doesn't take long to deteriorate. And much like everywhere else in the region in the year 1892, rumors from another century start spreading through the small village of Exeter, Rhode Island: vampires are responsible for all these deaths, to the point that people claim to have seen Mercy wandering around the crypt at night.

Popular pressure was so great that the father agreed to dig up his family's remains. Mercy's showed no signs of decomposition, and thus was she declared the culprit and submitted to the standard rituals performed on vampires: her heart and liver were torn out, then burned and mixed with water that was then given to Edwin to drink to ward off the influence of the living dead... but in vain. The boy succumbed only two months later. The last case of vampirism to be recorded in history, Mercy Brown's case was commented on extensively in the press at the time. The story traveled across the Atlantic to reach Bram Stoker, who was particularly inspired by it for one of the key scenes in his novel—when Van Helsing and his acolytes discover the intact remains of Lucy Westenra.

New GENERATION Vampires

IN 1895, THE LUMIÈRE BROTHERS invented the cinematograph, the essential tool in a cultural revolution that would shape the destiny of my people like nothing before it: film. The love affair between vampires and the "seventh art" was instantaneous. Our image was projected for you mortals on the big screen in every corner of the globe, united with the darkness you hold so dear. The big Hollywood studios seized on the figure of Dracula, making him popular well into the 2000s. The 20th century made us icons of pop culture. Always on the margins, of course, but listening out for the vibrations of an ever-changing world, we children of the night learned to adapt ourselves to better deceive our pray, and cheat the wearying solitude of immortality.

We now have a conscience, existential angst, and feelings of love, and are able to feed ourselves without killing. A new era has begun, and your fascination with us lives on, as eternal as our existence.

Dracula on screen, A TALE of love and blood

THE FIRST BIG VAMPIRE FILM in history saw the light of day in Germany in 1922, less than thirty years after the invention of cinema. Friedrich Murnau's *Nosferatu* is an unofficial adaptation of Bram Stoker's novel. A monstrous creature with a creepy silhouette, the vampire haunts the screen in a game of light and shadow as chilling as it is hypnotic. Still, it's on the other side of the Atlantic that Dracula becomes a star. In 1931, Hollywood seized on the figure of the count and dedicated to him talking cinema's first ever fantasy film: Tod Browning's *Dracula*. Moving away from Stoker's repulsive physical description, the actor Bela Lugosi gives him style and blesses him with his signature accessory, which will dwell in the collective imagination forever: his long cape. The count takes the United States by storm. America shivers with fear and delight at this predatory dandy with his pale face and biting smile. The film is a huge success, popularizing the character of Dracula throughout the world. Vampires modeled on Bela Lugosi make it into the canon of comics and pulp magazines, laying the ground for their return to haunt the dark rooms in the 1958 film *Dracula*, one of the first horror films in color. With Christopher Lee's portrayal, the film gives us a version of the count who is at once charismatic and bestial, all his teeth bared. The general fascination is multiplied ten times by the red of all that blood, splashed across the screen for the first time ever. In the two decades that follow, Dracula lives out his golden age, and genre cinema has eyes for him only.

Coppola's Dracula, the vampire tortured by his sins

IN HIS 1992 FILM, Francis Ford Coppola redefined the figure of the count by fleshing out his origin story. Distraught at the suicide of his beloved, abandoned by the Church which he still served, this Dracula renounced his faith and took a vow of eternal vengeance on all of humanity, turning into the bloodthirsty vampire we all know. The director also reinvented Mina Harker, so that she was now a reincarnation of Dracula's dead wife. Without losing Stoker's narrative structure, the film highlights the story of their love—as passionate as it was untenable. Dracula is now no longer just a cruel monster; he's a victim of his own madness in love. Rediscovering a humanity in him that makes him regret his terrible deeds, he ends up begging Mina to put an end to his tortured existence. A new ambiguity, then, which doesn't escape filmgoers, who find themselves struggling to celebrate the vampire's eventual death.

"'MINA, YOU'LL BE CURSED AS I AM TO WALK IN THE SHADOW OF DEATH FOR ALL ETERNITY. I LOVE YOU TOO MUCH TO CONDEMN YOU.'
'THEN TAKE ME AWAY FROM ALL THIS DEATH.'"
Dracula (Gary Oldman) and Mina Harker (Winona Ryder) in *Dracula* (dir. Francis Ford Coppola, 1992)

Down with Dracula: THE BIRTH of the modern vampire

1976 MARKS A NEW ERA for us vampires. In *Interview with the Vampire*, the first book in the thirteen *Vampire Chronicles*, Anne Rice will revolutionize our image, importantly having us shed our Christian heritage. From now on, it's only the light of the sun that can kill us, which restricts us to living at night. Better still, Rice literally gives us a voice in that first book, thanks to the character of Louis, precursor to a whole new generation of vampires.

In conversation with a journalist, Louis unfurls his whole life story, starting with his memories of being mortal and meeting his creator, Lestat. The vampire is no longer a demonic enemy, but a hero who can tell his own story. You'll find, dear humans, that he has a soul, and isn't necessarily condemned. Rather like you, he torments himself, searching for the meaning of his existence. And while Lestat embraces his bloodthirsty nature, Louis can't resolve himself to a life of killing, so much does he suffer from his own immortality. For Louis, a vampire among mortals, a mortal among vampires, the gift of darkness is a burden. An entire generation was inspired by Anne Rice's writing, and with her comes a new vampire code which relegates the figure of Count Dracula to the olden days. Ever adaptable to the times, the vampire evolves along with humans. Lestat even embarks on a career as a rockstar after he's revealed his true nature. Gone is the dusty old aristocrat; from now on, we're shockingly young and beautiful. It's an image we'll never shake.

"WHAT DOES IT MEAN TO DIE WHEN YOU CAN LIVE UNTIL THE END OF THE WORLD? AND WHAT IS 'THE END OF THE WORLD' EXCEPT A PHRASE, BECAUSE WHO KNOWS EVEN WHAT IS THE WORLD ITSELF?"

Anne Rice, *Interview With the Vampire* (1976)

From darkness TO LIGHT

WITH THE TV SERIES *Buffy the Vampire Slayer*, modern vampires make it into homes everywhere, and in the process enter people's hearts. In 2005, a romantic dream becomes a declaration of love with Stephenie Meyer's *Twilight* saga, books which then became films. The romance between a young human, Bella Swan, and an eternally teenage vampire, Edward Cullen, brings us closer to you humans than ever. Edward goes to school, doesn't fear the light of day, and comes from a family who have made a vow only to drink the blood of animals. In the wake of the *Twilight* phenomenon, stories about vampires and mortals invade the literary scene, to the point that an entire genre, "bit lit" (examples include *The Vampire Diaries* and *True Blood*) attracts fan communities from all over the world. Twenty-first-century vampires rediscover their human side, and it's this new conscience that gives us a choice our ancestors never had: to refuse to take life away from you to extend our own, and to do so without suffering for it. We will never be truly like you, but we have learned from you to love, and to integrate into your world, despite our dark side. Beneath our everlasting beauty, we can now feel the kind of passion that you do, and share with you a fragment of our own immortality. Dear mortals, our stories are now forever linked, and even if this endless existence sometimes brings me pain, I am rapt by curiosity as to what new ways you humans will come up with to reinvent us. After all, unlike the tombs in which we slept in days gone by, the great vampire myths are no longer set in stone—and that's what makes them so beautiful.

Buffy the stereotype slayer

IN BRAM STOKER'S NOVEL, Dracula shares his castle with "his" three vampire brides, who attempt to seduce Jonathan Harker so as to bring him down. But do you know their names? You can't: they don't have them. If the vampire is always a "he" in your imagination, it won't have escaped you that his victim, on the other hand, is almost always a "she." Women play the role of the young innocent who, if she becomes a vampire herself, transforms into a lascivious being, reduced to nothing but this sensuality.

At the dawn of the 21st century, two young heroines burst through this cliché and made our former nemesis, Professor Van Helsing, a figure of the past. Mixing different genres, Anita Blake from the literary saga of that name by Laurell K. Hamilton, and Buffy Summers from the TV series *Buffy the Vampire Slayer*, are formidable killers protecting the world from vampires of all kinds, as cruel as they are complex. *Buffy* was among the first to bring the myth of the vampire to the small screen, setting it in the world of teenagers.

"IN EVERY GENERATION, THERE IS A CHOSEN ONE. SHE ALONE SHALL STAND AGAINST THE VAMPIRES, DEMONS, AND FORCES OF DARKNESS. SHE IS THE SLAYER."

Tagline from *Buffy the Vampire Slayer*

Edward Cullen, the eternal Prince Charming

EDWARD CULLEN FROM *TWILIGHT* has no fear of the sun. Better yet, his skin lights up in it "as if it were encrusted with millions of diamonds," captivating Bella. The symbolism here is powerful: the vampire has turned his back on the shadows and transformed into an immortal Prince Charming, who makes teenage hearts turn somersaults. Bringing together two quite different themes, Stephenie Meyer redefined the image of the vampire and our place in the world. This transformation may be recent, but there's nothing modern about it, since Meyer is drawing from the courtly literature of the Middle Ages. There's the quest for eternal love, as well as the theme of the 'young old man', the teenager with centuries-old wisdom.

Adam and Eve, immortal lovers in a world of decline

ADAM AND EVE are the main characters in Jam Jarmusch's film *Only Lovers Left Alive* (2013). Immortal witnesses to the onward march of humanity, they have vowed to be faithful to each other as the centuries go by, and they work in secret to advance the scientific, literary, and artistic accomplishments of humanity, the mediocrity of which disgusts them. The mortals are meanwhile portrayed as greedy, grotesque and malevolent monsters, "zombies" who are poisoning even their own blood. The two vampires make an effort to bring them up to their level, as meanwhile Eve strives not to let Adam sink into weariness and contempt. Here we have a whole new side to the vampire myth, and a troubling role reversal.

Vampire SYMBOLS and Emblems

Garlic

Garlic has been growing in Europe for millennia. In the 1st century CE, Pliny the Elder had already noticed its power to protect against snake bites and scorpions, probably thanks to its strong odor. This property, mixed with antiseptic and purifying qualities, has elevated it to the status of protective plant in Eastern Europe, the Mediterranean Basin, and India. Garlic can ward off the evil eye (a supernatural curse in many cultures) and all kinds of harmful forces. This belief is particularly prevalent in certain Romanian villages, where strings of garlic are hung on doors and windows to protect all entryways.

Silver

In the eyes of the alchemist, gold and silver are the two "perfect" metals, as these were traditionally believed to be the only ones that can withstand the ravages of fire. This proves that their chemical composition is free of sulfur, an element particularly sensitive to flames, and thought to be impure. That's where we get the idea that a weapon made from one of these metals will be the most apt for fighting evil. Because of its color, silver has always evoked the moon and the nighttime, bringing together radiance and purity. It didn't take much for it to become, in the form of the silver bullet, the weapon of choice to use against werewolves and their cousin, the vampire.

Hawthorn

Its delicately scented white flowers have been a symbol of purity since antiquity, and its very sturdy wood makes for the vampire hunter's ideal stake. With their thorny branches, hawthorn bushes are perfect for planting a protective hedge. The Romans, who called the plant *alba*, meaning simply "white," had a custom of hanging a branch of hawthorn over the cradles of infants, to ward off the bite of the *strix*, a malevolent bird attracted to the blood of the young. The Roman poet Ovid bears witness to this in the following verse from his poem *Fasti*: "he gave her a thorn (it was whitethorn) / With which to drive away evil from the threshold."

The Vampire Ball

In several traditions, it's believed that vampires, like demons, come together on the night of a full moon. In Romania, on the night of St. George, the Vampire Ball takes place, a party in which vampires are for once allowed to eat a bit of human food. In Eastern Europe, there's Walpurgis Night, "when, according to the belief of millions of people, the devil was abroad—when the graves were opened and the dead came forth and walked. When all evil things of earth and air and water held revel," as described by Bram Stoker. Celebrated every April 30th, this is an ancient pagan festival dedicated to the end of winter, which carries on in secret despite the prohibition by the Catholic Church, which strove to associate it with the witches' sabbath.

Mist

Many different powers have been attributed to the vampire, of which one is controlling natural events like gales and thunderstorms, or transforming into a shadowy mist. In this weightless form, the vampire can easily escape his tomb, travel at an incredible speed and plunge the world into a dark and anxious mood—the perfect conditions for terrible crimes.

Canines

The sharpest teeth in the human mouth. These are particularly developed in predators, as their function is to tear meat. While today these are the arguably the vampire's most defining feature, they didn't appear in folklore until relatively recently. The original vampire myths have vampires sucking their victims' skin, rather than biting: the belief was that they fed themselves through the victim's pores. It wasn't until the 19th century that canines were mentioned, first in a pulp journal featuring Varney the vampire, who has "fearful-looking teeth—projecting like those of some wild animal, hideously, glaringly white, and fang-like." In the century that followed, Dracula and Carmilla were given long and pointed canines. Cinema took care of the rest...

Coffin

In ancient times, you hunted a vampire down to his tomb. His monstrous figure would appear when you opened the coffin, often covered in blood, sometimes with a chunk of shroud half-chewed in his mouth. Either way, a terrible sight to behold. It seems like a natural move for the modern vampire to sleep in a coffin, even if it hasn't always been the case. What better place to shelter from the brightness of daylight?

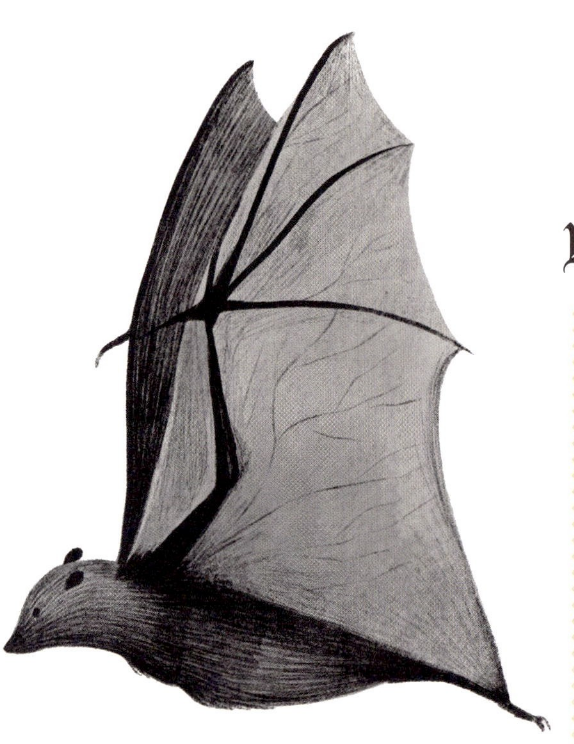

Bat

In 1810, scientists officially described a new species of subtropical bat, armed with long canines and keen on animal blood: the "vampire bat." Leaving aside the specifics of this precise variety, the bat has always suffered a bad reputation. A land mammal equipped with black wings, the bat has a dual identity and, as a result, is much feared. Incapable of graceful flight, its chaotic flapping gives it the appearance of a failed bird, a condemned soul. Winning the contest between animals that are somewhat disgraced in the public imagination (spiders and moths, for example), the bat has, over time, become the trademark vampiric creature.

Cross

Catholic religion paints vampires like other demons—as blasphemous imitations of Christ. Hardly surprising, then, that vampires fear holy water, sacramental bread, and, of course, the cross—that central symbol of Christianity, which conjures both the redemption and sacrifice of Christ and divine eternity. In *An Examen of Witches*, Henry Boguet gives very precise descriptions of how to identify someone who's had dealings with the devil, among them the fact of not wearing a cross on one's rosary.

Daylight

Vampires are creatures of shadow and night. Like nightmares that dissolve at the first glimmers of dawn, they can only flourish in darkness, that realm of the imagination unhampered by the hubbub of daytime. The effect of daylight, the vampire's sworn enemy, is, however, different depending on what story you encounter. Traditionally, it simply *limited* the vampire's powers. It wasn't until 1922 that the sun's destructive power materialized, in Friedrich Murnau's beautiful *Nosferatu*.

Wolf

Wild animal, symbol of that which can't be tamed, the wolf is as intriguing as it is terrifying. Its howling at the sky and nighttime excursions have made us associate it with the moon, and its supposed bloodlust, hated by shepherds whose flocks have been attacked, hasn't much improved its reputation. Vampires, bestial by nature, have the gift of communicating with and taming these wild animals. This is particularly so in the case of Dracula, who claims to revel in their howl: "Listen to them—the children of the night. What music they make!"

Shadow

Like their reflection, the shadow represents the part of the soul that has been lost by the vampire. Stripped of his spiritual elements, the vampire is nothing but a one-dimensional body, brought to life by evil and unable to project or reflect itself.

Stake

The weapon of choice for getting rid of a vampire. Most of the time, the stake is not enough to completely destroy a vampire; it simply serves to halt him while the executioner rips out his heart or cuts off his head. Only purifying fire can permanently get rid of evil. In parts of rural Romania, there are documented cases of people driving stakes preventatively through the bodies of some of the dead—the ones who seem liable to come back to vampirize the living. The type of wood is very important. It has to be particularly hard or come from a fruit-bearing tree, a symbol of life. That's why apple and hawthorn stakes are considered the most effective.

Dust

Since the living dead have generally outlived their allotted time on Earth, it seems natural that the vampire should turn to dust when he's destroyed, as though time were regaining its hold on matter. This image is nevertheless a fairly recent one, and comes largely from *Buffy the Vampire Slayer*. In ancient times, a vampire who had been pierced by a stake would collapse on himself with a cavernous sound as soon as the fresh blood of his victims had left his body.

Rats

Teeming and nocturnal, rats are associated with clandestine, nefarious activity. Often thought of as invasive, and disease-carrying creatures, the fear and disgust they inspire in humans has a xenophobic tinge: the hatred of the rat is like the hatred of the other, the "foreigner" who is imagined arriving en masse and being the source of all problems. The characters of Dracula and Nosferatu are each the image of a supposedly barbarous outsider, bringing terror and plague to a hushed and civilized world. Of course, each is followed by his army of rats.

Reflection

In many cultures, the mirror is a symbol of truth. The reflection it shows us, pure and lacking ulterior motives, is thought to reveal the very essence of a person, their soul. Often present in Western storytelling, in *Snow White* it discloses to the wicked stepmother that her young stepdaughter surpasses her in beauty. No mirror can show the vampire's reflection, since he's only an image, cut off from his soul. It seems that Bram Stoker was the first to make mention of this.

Blood

Were we to run out of it, we'd die. Red and warm, it symbolizes everything related to heat, and is universally considered our life force, so much so that in certain religions, to consume it is forbidden. Unlike breath, the vehicle of spiritual life, blood is intimately associated with flesh, with the body: it's the most tangible and sensual expression of life. Some cultures believe blood can create life when mixed with soil, and of course, it is what brings the bodily husks of the undead back to life.

Birthplace

The idea that the vampire needs to stay in his birthplace or risk being weakened comes from Bram Stoker's *Dracula*. That novel lists a great number of limits to the power of the prince of darkness: Dracula can't enter another's home without having first been invited inside, he can only sleep on consecrated ground, and cannot cross running water... The principle of the strength-giving birthplace surely comes from ancient legends of a patriotic nature—those that associate power with native land.

Poppy seeds

In several cultures, the vampire comes up against an astonishing limitation: faced with a pile of seeds or other grains, he can't help but undertake to count every single one. In Chinese tradition, the *jiangshi* is obliged to count every grain if a bag of rice is opened in his path. In Romania even today, if a dead person is thought to be liable to come back to haunt the living, people will sometimes leave a pouch filled with poppy seeds or small pebbles on the corpse's chest, to divert their attention. In the same spirit, people also say that a revenant can't help but try and undo a knot if they see one. That's why a knotted rope is often found in a vampire-hunter's arsenal.

Salt

An imperishable substance, salt has been used for millennia for preserving food. That's largely why it has acquired such a privileged status: because it prevents things from perishing, we associate it with purity, even sometimes with immortality. That's why you might form a protective circle or barrier of salt, to ward off bad things.

Talons

In *Dracula*, the narrator mentions that the Count's nails are long and pointed. Modern vampires are still very often given this feature, their sharp nails serving the same predatory function as an animal's claws—to rip apart their prey. These "human claws" embody the cross between man and beast that's typical of many vampire tendencies. In less common versions of the vampire myth, the vampire is sometimes characterized by his excessive hairiness, which is why the monobrow has for a while been one of his distinctive features.

GLOSSARY

acolyte An assistant or follower.
alchemist Someone who practices alchemy, a type of medieval chemistry that aimed to turn materials to gold.
ambivalent Having feelings that contradict each other.
antiseptic Able to prevent the growth of germs that cause disease.
apparition A ghost or ghostlike illusion.
arsenal A collection of equipment or weapons.
barbarous Uncivilized.
bestial Having the qualities of an animal.
blasphemous Disrespectful toward God or something sacred.
canon A list of works of art considered to be the best and most worthwhile in their category.
clergyman A male priest or religious leader.
contagion The spreading of disease.
credulous Too ready to believe things.
dandy A stylish and fashionable man, especially in the 19th century.
delegation A group of people who represent another person, nation, or organization.
demonology The study of demons.
diabolical Having the qualities of the devil.
disabuse Persuade someone that they are mistaken about something.
envoy A person who represents a nation in official business.
epicenter The central point of something.
epidemic A widespread disease in a particular place.
existential Concerned with the existence of something.
exorcism An attempt to remove an evil spirit from a person or place.
genetic Relating to genes, the qualities passed down from parents to children.
gladiator In ancient Rome, someone trained to fight for entertainment.
hallucination The experience of seeing or hearing something that is not really there.
ideological Relating to the principles of a particular organization.
immortality The ability to live forever.
Inquisition, the The institutions within the Catholic Church, set up in the 13th century, whose purpose was to remove those who disagreed with Catholic teachings.
lycanthropy The condition of being a werewolf, or of believing oneself to be a werewolf.
macabre Disturbing due to a relationship with death.
Mesoamerica A cultural region in southern North America and Central America.
Mesopotamia A region of Asia between the Tigris and Euphrates rivers.
meticulous Showing attention to detail.
mutation The changing of a gene.
ointment An oily paste used in medicine.
pagan Having religious beliefs other than those of recognized religions.
pantheon The gods and goddesses of a religion.
pestiferous Bringing disease.
pestilence A fatal disease.
pre-Columbian Relating to the history, culture, and peoples of North and South America before the Italian explorer Christopher Columbus arrived there in 1492.
precursor Something that comes before another of its kind.
putrefaction The process of decay in a body.
Renaissance, the A historical period in Europe from the 14th to the 16th centuries.
revenant Someone who has returned from the dead.
rosary A string of beads used in the Rosary, a set of Catholic prayers.
sacramental Relating to something that has a role in a religious ritual.
scapegoat Someone blamed for the mistakes of others because it is easier to blame that person.
Sultan The title given to the ruler of the Ottoman Empire, which existed from the 14th to the 20th centuries.
talisman An object thought to have magical powers.
vagabond Someone who wanders between places, with no home or job.
vagary An unexpected change.
veritable Truly being something or having a particular quality.
xenophobic Having a hatred against people from other countries.